MW01601867

Engaging

the Gospel of Mary Magdalene

by

Kim Beyer

ISBN: 9781798117460

Copyright 2019 Kimberly Beyer

All rights reserved.

No part of this book may be used or reproduced in any manner whatsoever without written permission except in cases of brief quotations embodied in critical articles and reviews

Cover design: Kim Beyer

Acknowledgements:

In memory of Sue Sutherland-Hanson,

who built her life around poetry,

her husband's gardens,

and teaching others about embodied Christianity.

You are deeply missed.

Thanks goes to my long-time buddy and fellow comparative religion junkie, Rev. Kayle Rice, who took the time to comb through this text.

Any remaining issues are wholly my own.

You May Also Enjoy These Titles

by

Kim Beyer

The Hidden Message of the Lost Gospel of Thomas:
Exploring the Ancient Practice of Unitive Christianity
w/ front cover blurb by Richard Rohr

Easing into the Gospel of Thomas

At Matthew's Knee: A Poetic Commentary on the Gospel of
Matthew, Volume 1

An Invitation to Openness
w/author Rev. Sue Sutherland Hanson

Introduction

The *Gospel of Mary Magdalene* (and the *Gospel of John* from our modern Bible) was penned in what most scholars identify as the 3rd century CE. Fragments have turned up over the years—tantalizing scraps of a once widely read and copied manuscript. Unlike some Gnostic texts which create a fantastic cosmology, this small piece of writing bridges vision and reality, captures the tension between a patriarchal culture and a woman who is sometimes called the Apostle to the Apostles. It also explores the very real death of Rabbi Yeshua (we know this man by his Western name, *Jesus*) and his continued spiritual presence in the consciousness of his disciples. It is curiously "alive" and filled with strong emotion, as well as metaphysical depth.

I find myself in the good company of translators like Stephen Mitchell or Coleman Barks, working with ancient words and breathing a modern life into them. While this might not be a wholly scholarly approach, it does allow the reader to better engage the living spirit of this gospel. If you peruse Amazon and check out how many "versions" of the classical Bible exist, perhaps you will understand the need to draw classical literature forward into our time and culture, so its message stays fresh and relevant. The Sources for Further Inquiry, listed at the end of this slim book, all served as my translation touchstones.

As with my book about the Gospel of Thomas, *Yeshua's Yoga*, I translate each saying in the Gospel of Mary Magdalene, using Jean Yves-LeLoup's manner of page and line for citation. I then write a short essay about the passage, followed by an original poem that captures the "spirit" of the text. Finally, I pose five study questions to ponder with others or in your journal. I highly recommend creating artwork with this gospel and will drop in suggestions about how to allow this work to unfold through music, dance, and visual media. I've also included a short and accessible resource page at the end of the work to further your study of this complex and beautiful piece of ancient writing. Scripture of any kind is meant to be chewed with your whole being. I am challenging you to relate these pages to your past and your own evolving journey in a way both deep and intimate.

Blessings on each step you take!

Kim Beyer

Chapter 1

Beginning with Ellipses

The Gospel of Mary Magdalene begins with what is not there—all our copies unearthed to date do not include the first six sayings. We begin, in other words, with a mystery. The first four chapters are missing, despite both Greek and Coptic archeological finds of the work discovered at Oxyrhynchus in Egypt, the *Berlin Gnostic Codex* (*Papyrus Berolinensis 8502*) discovered in Akhmim in upper Egypt and later inserted by scholars in collected works of the Nag Hammadi Codex.

The number of excavated fragments of this text point to the fact it was widely copied and disseminated across the Eastern edge of a young Christian movement. Copying was time and labor intensive, and multiple copies means the text was important to early Christians. Like the *Gospel of Thomas*, this work may have never made the Council of Nicea's cutting table, where the material of the modern Bible was selected and given the Roman Church's stamp of approval. Or if it had indeed been considered, its teaching, delivered by a woman, and based on a visionary event, may have discomforted the patriarchal leadership of a religion poised to become the official church of the patriarchal Roman empire.

The missing chapters are an invitation to the modern seeker, though. They give us the "space" necessary to tap into the mood of the work which will begin with teachings from the risen Yeshua delivered to his frightened and confused disciples after the crucifixion. They create a mystery upon mystery, a liminal space, a threshold and questions that open us all to the unfolding teaching of both Mary and the man we call Jesus.

Poetic Response:

Sitting with the Missing Sayings 1-6

No, don't dig too deeply here.

Hold the silence, the possibility,

and allow this mystery to serve

as the beginning place.

So often, we rush,

tumbling over words,

making connections and judgements,

asking questions that

prove a point we've already chosen.

Be still.

Let yourself find a place in the Great Circle of life,

and discover ears that hear.

Engaging the Text:

1. How do you feel about beginning with a text that is missing its first four chapters? What did you notice about thoughts that arose within you or any visceral responses to what was not there?

2. How might you capture the ellipses in visual art? In music? How can you dance what is not there, setting the mood?

3. Take the time to go on the internet and look at pictures of the *Gospel of Mary Magdalene's* Greek and Coptic fragments. How did you respond to the images? To the stories about how they were found?

4. As you start this study, what biases or expectations are flavoring your adventure? List them and consider their source. For instance, perhaps you can feel a wary distrust of this text because Mary Magdalene has been portrayed as a sinner and harlot in your religious educational past. How does this affect how you read this scripture?

5. Do some online research about how Mary Magdalene was portrayed through time by Christianity, her place in the Bible and as a saint. Create a list of her many faces (or even an art collage of her representations through time) and refer to it as you continue to read this Gospel.

Chapter 2

Translation:

The disciples asked the risen Yeshua, "...will matter be utterly destroyed, then? What is its nature?"

Yeshua answered, "Every composite piece of matter exists in a web of relationship and is structured from that web. As matter dissolves, it will return to its root Source, according to its inherent nature. Those who have ears, let them hear."

(Page 7, 1-9)

Musings:

We enter the dialogue with Yeshua mid-stream, without any narrative support to give us the place, the time and so forth. Who is present? What prompted this line of questioning? Only as we continue from this point, do we come to understand this is the classical appearance of Jesus after his death on the cross. He is answering the last questions from his disciples and preparing them to go forth and preach his message before he departs.

They have seen their master die. Yet here he stands, answering their questions. It seems quite in keeping then that the question about the nature of physical matter would be forefront on the minds of the rabbi's students.

The answer Yeshua provides is a complex one. Matter does not exist in isolation. Like the Buddhist concept of "interdependent co-arising", matter hangs on matter, a web of relationship that both binds and supports the material world. What can be created, born, constructed and so forth will, by its own nature, fall apart again. Yet, Yeshua points beyond the physical to the Source or Root that supports and informs the web of the material universe. There is an unchanging base beneath the play of what Indian philosophers called "maya" or the illusion of the physical world.

If you consider your hand, you will notice that each finger and the thumb seem to have a separate existence—you can name them, some have jewelry they sport, maybe each nail is painted in a unique fashion. But if you were to lose a finger, would you still have a hand? The myriad faces of Matter, like the fingers, seem separate and individualistic, yet on another level, taken together they make up "hand-ness". Matter can be broken down further and further, from hand to fingers, to specific joints and tendons and bones of a finger, nails, to the network of specific muscles and veins, to the cells creating the working parts of the digit, to the mitochondrial energy fueling those cells, smaller and smaller bits of matter working in a networked relationship. But expanding, the finger is part of the hand, which is part of the right or left arm, which belongs to the right or left side of a body, which takes membership in hundreds of relational activities...mother, daughter, grandma, writer, artist, US citizen, citizen of earth, on and on. What is the Real? It must be something beyond the merely *conceptual idea* or name that allows us to label each level of "hand" and think we know it.

Yeshua points to the idea that what is a composite (which is everything in the universe, including you) will break down and decompose into its base, its Source, its root. And what is that? What upholds this continuous flow of the building blocks of matter constantly creating relationships of complexity and falling apart again? What is the bowl that holds such unceasing and wonderful change?

Paul said God is "that in which we live and move and have our being," (Acts 17:28). Yeshua seems to be alluding to a similar idea: when matter breaks completely down, we find the root that is God. The Divine is both the bowl and the space sustaining the soup-elements of matter's intimate relationships. It is the web of interrelationships, giving life and structure to the building blocks of reality.

Countless times, this cup has shattered,

broken itself on stone, on wood,

on someone's clumsy foot.

I have swept dust up from its firing,

drank the water of its birth,

lay on the hillside of hard-baked summer clay

when it hadn't yet dreamed of form.

I have digested with its glazing fire,

wondered about the usefulness of emptiness

as I stirred coffee into its belly,

laughed at the clever leaning "Nobody is Perfect"

reincarnation of its mug-ness.

Pour the wine now—

can you keep the seams from dripping?

Don't try!

Communion flows like that.

Engaging the Text:

1. How does the way Yeshua speak about matter compare to modern physics? Take some time and explore some basic concepts about the nature of matter on the internet!

2. If you could ask the risen Yeshua a question, what would it be? Or would you want to engage with him through language at all? Explain.

3. How do you explain the presence of Yeshua if matter breaks down, returning to its source? What do you believe happens to matter? What is its Source or "nature"?

4. Do you believe you can experience your Source or Root while alive? How?

5. Explore the many ways that matter is connected as a web of relationships. What are the ramifications of your exploration for the way you live and interact with all of matter?

Chapter 3

Translation:

Peter asked him, "you have been explaining everything we have asked of you. Can you answer this, then? What great sin imprisons this world?"

Yeshua replied, "There is no such Reality as sin. You all produce this idea when you act as if you are the only subject in a world of objects. This is called sin. This is why relational Good has entered into your lives, in presence and in action, so that you might remember your Source and Root."

(Page 7, Lines 9-22)

Musings:

I wonder why, with the Good amongst them again, the disciples fall back to question after question, locking themselves into their logical minds when a miracle stands before them. Perhaps this is part of how we "control" situations, reducing them to ideas that can be manipulated. When Peter asks about sin with a kind of capital "S", Yeshua is quick to pull the rug out from under him by replying the concept itself has no reality—it's an *idea* alone, a mistake of equating a name or label with knowing.

Humans create consensual reality by naming it. Think back to Genesis, when Adam is asked to name all of creation. Each strand of the web of existence was already there, but each name separated and individualized each small piece of the web of life, making it sacred and seen. Naming, though, is both gift and curse because, on one hand, a name allows us to engage Being to Being with what might otherwise be simply an object. But on the other hand, a name will sometimes bar the way to deeper knowing. If I say the name "crow", then you think you know what I am talking about. Crow is the label or tag you use for those elegant black birds with the ragged and throaty cries. However, you miss the "crow-ness" of this individual bird, with his scarred beak and the missing flight feather in his right wing. When we name, we think we know.

Yeshua points out that the Good has illuminated the lives of the disciples, both in action and presence, to show them a different kind of consciousness, one based on relationship. As Martin Buber said in *I and Thou*, "All real living is meeting."

This meeting, this relational aspect of life that Yeshua calls "Good", does more than bind matter to matter in the great web of being. It also reminds humans of their Root and Source, the unitive consciousness that is the bowl, of a God who flows and is the flow through that web of relationships. This is our ultimate Source and Root, and we participate always in "God-ness" when we cease dividing the world into subject and objects.

Responsive Poem:

Come, put your back against this trunk.

No, don't name it "birch"

or begin to talk about how you remember

its leaves glowing amber

in the fall light.

Stop layering memory on top of right now,

and reach out with every sense.

Touch the bits of the tree strewn about you,

like the mail found by the new puppy,

the scent of years of decay tenderly midwifing life,

the sound of a northern wind

drawing music from black, naked branches.

Fall and fall into tree-ness,

until your spine is fused with

roots and trunk and

motion stirring the gray sky.

Engaging the Text:

1. Set three objects on the table. Take a sheet of paper and name each one. Then, begin to explore each object with all your senses. When you have finished (take your time!), create a poem about the objects that illustrates what you have discovered about each. You may want to create new names for each piece, to remind yourself this is not simply a "bowl" or a "tooth-brush". How would your life be different if you took the time to deeply engage with what you "think" you know about matter, even periodically?

2. Do you ever find asking questions to "hang onto" or cling to someone as an object, using questions to distance yourself, place yourself "higher" or "lower than" the person before you? Consider the polite "cocktail" conversation or even some Facebook encounters. Are these truly relational or merely the façade of it?

3. The word sin is often translated as "missing the mark". How does this definition change the passage we are considering?

4. In the Hindu tradition, the "root" of being embodied is considered to be joy—that sense that "all shall be well, and all shall be well, and all manner of things shall be well," that Julian of Norwich found. How does that concept of joy as our root illuminate the passage we are working with?

5. How much of modern Christianity, in its many forms, ask us to ground our lives in the root or source of Being? Define Root or Source for yourself and create a list of how traditional churches ask us to reconnect with this concept. What else could they do in congregations to explore and actualize this idea?

Chapter 4

Translation:

Yeshua continued speaking. "You get sick and you die because you cling to a reality that is not true. If you are a thinking person, you should consider this."

(Page 7, line 23-28)

Musings:

Here in the West, we've developed a strange tradition in some circles to blame illness and death on wrong thinking, failure to forgive, frustrated dreams, wrong relationships with God, on and on. I recall a story from my holistic health program days at Western University. Bernie Seigel, MD, was working with the role of stress as the root of illness. He had been asked to present a workshop, and the turnout was huge. He started this way:

"Everyone who runs at least a mile a day, stand up!" Parts of the crowd proudly leapt to their feet.

"Everyone who only eats vegetarian cuisine, stand up!" Other folks joined the ones standing.

"People who take vitamins and only use holistic health modalities, stand up!" More folks bounced eagerly to their feet.

He went on like this for some time, until every special diet, exercise, meditation style and so forth had been rousingly spoken. He paused then, gazing out on the crowd with a little smile on his face.

"You're all gonna die. Sit down!"

Yes, I imagine there was a stunned moment of silence then nervous laughter. But the good doctor had poked the elephant in the room right in his nose—all of us, at some point, will either have an accident or get ill and die. All of us.

So, what is Yeshua trying to convey here? He knows very well that all things grow sick and die—he's the risen Christ, and he's been through the whole ugly scene of sufferings, loss and death.

Recall in the previous chapter that Yeshua pointed out that all matter essentially falls apart, its pieces re-entering the dynamic stream of the Root or Source of all created things. The Good Teacher is not speaking of illness and death as terminal events here, as a line from birth to illness or trauma and then death. That's the small way of thinking. He's calling his disciples to consider that their *concepts* of illness and death as ending places, as concrete ideas even, is faulty reasoning.

In the *Heart Sutra* of Buddhism, we hear a similar note:

> *"...Listen Sariputra,*
> *this Body itself is Emptiness*
> *and Emptiness itself is this Body.*
> *This Body is not other than Emptiness*
> *and Emptiness is not other than this Body.*
> *The same is true of Feelings,*
> *Perceptions, Mental Formations,*
> *and Consciousness..."*

(Translation by Thich Nhat Hahn)

It's not that death and illness aren't *relatively* real. We have been to funerals and seen the coffins. We've been sick or know people who have been ill. But that's only one side of the picture. Yeshua points out the Source, the Root, *is* Ultimate Reality. Yes, *matter falls apart, but then it returns to its Beginning Place*. So what dies? What is ill? He's asking his students to grow beyond the small definitions of these words.

He's also using the concepts of illness and death in a very clever way—our inability to hold both relative and ultimate reality in our consciousness IS an illness and a kind of death. We cannot love completely and well when we are capable of only standing in relative reality (or in ultimate reality for that matter). Our ability to create meaningful and creative relationships become stunted because we strive to protect ourselves from pain, when we grasp onto matter as something unending and eternal in and of itself. This is an illness, and eventually, it's a kind of death. We die to the larger and richer world that Yeshua perceives. That's why he calls his disciples to consider his words deeply—get beyond the concept and see the larger landscape of Reality.

Responsive Poem:

In a meditation,

I journeyed to the bedside of my dying self.

"Based on what you know now,

what should I be doing with my life?"

I asked.

It was a Big Question,

and at thirty years old,

I wanted Big Answers.

My older self merely smiled and held out her hand.

A broken Ph.D. frame hung askew on the wall by her head,

When I looked at it, frowning,

she squeezed my fingers, just enough,

to return my gaze to her eyes.

I'm still learning to have ears that hear.

Engaging the Text:

1. Today, one of the gifts we have been given is access to many cultural and traditional "ways" of engaging with Reality. It's also one of the difficult elements of being alive—learning to discern what path and nature of Ultimate reality speaks to us. Take a moment today, and muse about what elements have gone into your upbringing, study and experiences that help you define your Source or Root within.

2. Create a picture or piece of writing that captures both the reality of illness and death as well as the idea that these are not necessarily terminal events. What did your creative work teach you?

3. Consider in your journal or in dialogue the impact of speaking with a being who has "risen" from death. Do you feel this was an actual event or a metaphor? Where do your opinions arise from?

4. What are the ramifications for humans when they can truly understand that death and illness are part of relative reality? Why do you think many people fear illness and death? What part does that "fear" have in how people create and maintain relationships with both other people and institutions and "tribes" like sports teams, churches and service organizations?

5. If you could journey in your mind to the bedside of your dying self, what questions would you ask? Do you think the questions you asked at 20 or 30 would be different from what you formulate at 50, 60 or 70? Explain.

Chapter 5

Translation:

"When you cling to matter alone, you miss the Source and Root. Your whole body then falls into confusion. Choose instead to find your still point in manifestations of that fuller image of nature around and within you. Those who have ears, let them hear."

(Page 8, Lines 1-10)

Musings:

If you remember the intimate resurrection scene between Mary and Jesus, he tells her "…do not cling to me, for I have not yet ascended to my Father. Rather, go and find our brethren and tell them I am ascending to my father and to your Father, to my God and your God." (John 20:17). When we hear again this Gospel, which scholars believe was contemporaneous with the Gospel of Mary Magdalene, we are granted a bi-focal vision into the mystery that should be at the heart of Christianity—a deeper understanding of incarnational theology.

In John, Jesus gently turns Mary's first response of clinging to his physical form back to the spiritual, even as he stands beside her, newly arisen from the grave. Matter and Source are held for a moment in perfect tension. The individuals themselves are in dynamic relationship with each other with ties that transcend the concept of Matter. They are indeed two, but united in the Father, in God, with all of Matter.

We begin to break through to a new way of seeing Reality. Rather than Yeshua alone holding the tension of divinity and matter in his form, the whole of creation participates in this new consciousness that sees both Matter and its Source in a single glance. His way of relating to divinity is an invitation for us to do the same—his father, his God, his way of being in the world can also be ours.

But the Gospel of Mary Magdalene points out that we must get used to the new bi-focals! This is an entirely new paradigm, one that the *Gospel of Thomas,* written in a very similar vein, claims will trouble us for a while until we break through and begin to hold both views. Then, we will be called to Stand up into that Cosmos, in time learning to both reign and rest. However, if we see only the Divine or only matter, the cost is nothing less than confusion through our whole body. Matter without Source falls apart. That perception of linear time, of dissolution, is the very root of much of our human suffering. But it is equally true that Source without dynamic Matter is inert, non-creative and lifeless. Matter expresses the Source, birthing an energy generated between subject and subject that in turn creates endlessly in a manner that is holy. Only when the two are held, Matter and Source, like lovers, does the deeper meaning of incarnation becomes accessible to us all.

We access the Root in stillness but manifest it in the activity of Matter. Then, all our activity becomes a mirror image of the Source. It's a dance of love and we are being asked to birth this new way of seeing.

Responsive Poem:

I gaze at the Tibetan Yidam,

smiling at how the dusty statue of physical passion

speaks also of the wild penetration of

Compassion into Wisdom,

Wisdom wrapping Compassion,

bonded in a

face to face embrace of equals.

Show me compassion that only sits on its hands.

Show me wisdom that throws itself into motion all the time--

when I find such things,

they are usually caricatures,

off-balance and illusory.

No, I resonate with this messy image

of Compassion kissing Wisdom,

for it echoes of

of Matter swirling around the Source,

of Sufis whirling about their Sheikhh,

of a lover passionately embracing the beloved.

Engaging the Text:

1. Create a piece of art, a dance or poem that captures the dynamic interplay of Matter and Source. What did your artwork reveal to you?

2. Why do you think the human mind holds separate the concept of "matter" and "the Source?" How is this a natural part of how the brain itself functions? How is it cultural? What are the ramifications of uniting these two separate realities?

3. What does the term "incarnation" mean to you? How has your definition(s) changed through time?

4. If you have a chance, read the Gospel of John and the Gospel of Mary Magdalene. In what ways do they share a common theology? In what ways are they different?

5. How do you think not seeing both Matter and Source bonded together creates trouble for your physical self? What about the "body of Christ" we have been exposed to in theological discourse? How does this "not seeing" affect your larger environment?

Chapter 6

Translation:

Yeshua, after he had spoken, addressed them all, saying, "Peace be with you. Find my peace within yourselves."

(Page 8, Lines 11-14)

Musings:

Reading to this point, have you asked yourself if Yeshua is materially in the room with his students? Is this a shared vision of him? Is this a narrative device, setting the reader up for the teachings Mary Magdalene will soon deliver?

Or perhaps this is a form of shamanic-style manifestation, brought about by accessing the consciousness that finds Yeshua's "peace within yourselves." (He'll make this even more clear in the next lines of page 8.)

In core shamanism (the basic technique of accessing levels of non-consensual reality), practitioners note that they are working with real entities on real levels of existence, usually an upper world, a middle world, and a lower world. The upper world is the realm of angels, wisdom spirits, and divine beings. The middle realm is thinly laid over our own, a level where the shaman can seek what is lost as well as speak to the many individual spirits of rocks, trees and so forth. The underworld is not a place. It's not the realm of death or evil, but rather the level where the deep intuitive function of mind resides as ancestors and the helping spirits.

As we shall see later, Mary relates a vision of Yeshua that certainly falls into the category of Semitic Shamanism. It's a kind of consciousness that is not like a night time dream, nor a day-dream, nor mere imagination. I wanted to bring this up now, so you have time to research shamanism a bit and compare it to the upcoming chapters.

At the very least, you'll recognize the lines we're considering today from John 14:27, another reason why scholars consider these two gospels to be from the same time period.

Because Yeshua has already taught that Matter falls apart, dissolving back into its Root or Source, he is leaving his students a clue about how to access him—through actions and states of mind that closely echo his own. His teachings have been a timeless gift, an energy that both confers his presence and calls the students into a consciousness like that of their teacher. That consciousness is by no means passive—it is a Way, a mode of creatively engaging our consensual reality that is fresh and alive.

Notice that this is not the stuff of simple belief in a teacher. It's an emulation and call to BE the teacher. There is no sweeter reward for such behaviors than peace—the peace that is based not on hope or rose-colored glasses, but a profound mix of compassion, detachment (in a healthy manifestation of that concept) and a new way of comprehending reality.

Responsive Poem:

I have listened to hundreds of sermons,

sat with Buddhists in meditation,

walked between worlds dancing on a drumbeat thread,

folded my body in Hatha Yoga asanas,

practiced Centering Prayer, Tonglen, mindfulness

on my square elephant cushion.

I've passed beads through my fingers,

paced the circuits of the labyrinth,

flowed through the forms of Qigong,

walked with my camera through a silent wood,

water colored trees on cold white tile

and let my flute suggest melodies to my fingers.

I have ridden lonely forest trails on horseback,

swam in the cold, tugging rivers,

sang Edelweiss on a high hill in Australia.

Folding laundry today,

I am simply

Peace.

Engaging the Text:

1. What levels of consciousness do you access each day? For instance, you might start your list with daydreaming or "worrying" which is engagement with a possibility, a thought-form. Are you startled by how many kinds of "reality" you engage in? Where does Communion fall in this list? What do YOU think is happening in this Rite?

2. Why are some kinds of consciousness viewed with suspicion in your culture? When did this suspicion first arise in history? Do your homework!

3. How do you define the word "peace"? Is it dynamic or very still? Is it something that can be shared or wholly personal? Be as creative and concrete as you can.

4. Based on your definition, can peace be "given" to someone? If so, how is this done? What are the ramifications for peace either being intensely personal, corporate or both?

5. Talk a bit about how you see the risen Yeshua in this text—is he "there" materially, as a memory, as a vision or a shamanic shared reality? Be willing to avoid clinging to any one "traditional" answer!

Chapter 7

Translation:

Yeshua said, "remain in a state of conscious discernment, so that you aren't fooled by people saying, 'the Teacher is here' or 'no, he's over there.' I, the Son of Humanity, exist within you and guide you. If you search for my presence, you will find it there.

Walk forth and spread this news about the kingdom. But do not create any new laws or rules beyond what I have shared with you or you will be ruled and dominated by them."

After he shared these last insights, he took his leave of them.

(Page 8, 15-24 and Page 9, 1-5)

Musings:

The first part of this teaching, about how to access both the Kingdom and Yeshua's presence, also shows up in the Gospel of Thomas, Logion 3 and in Luke 17:20-21. Please do read both these renditions and compare them to this passage from the Gospel of Mary Magdalene. Taken together, they comprise a powerful statement about how to be in relationship with Yeshua.

First, we must actively seek his presence or the Kingdom ourselves. We must do the work. As we are told in the Gospel of Thomas, those who Search *will* Find (Logion 2). When we choose to discern, to look deeply into consensual reality, we break through to Ultimate Reality. Then, we walk the Kingdom as Yeshua did. (Compare this idea to "not I, but Christ who lives in me" in Galatians 2:20.)

This level of consciousness is sometimes referred to as the *imaginal* realm, and it is neither a day dream, a vision or imagination per se. Why do I make this distinction? Because accessing the Teacher and the Way he viewed the world is a transformational experience for us. We are changed, at a very deep level, and it begins with our own efforts to create the relationship.

Second, *harkening to folks trying to point us toward "their" Yeshua or Kingdom is not the same as directly experiencing the Master or his Reality ourselves.* He's trying to point out that our personal contact with Presence is more critical than believing what other people try to convey. This calls to question any religious teaching that places the primacy on scriptural belief, tradition, or institutional dogmas rather than the living experience of Yeshua and the Kingdom. Why? Because a belief is not the same as being in relationship with Yeshua, and we are fundamentally changed within by relationship rather than thoughts, laws, traditions or ethical rules.

Speaking of rules and laws, Yeshua points out for the second time in this document that essentially sin is *created* when you look for it and make it real. It's also true that the more rules and laws you add, the stronger you make consensual and relative reality and the more you are pulled from Presence and into institutionalism, division and duality. For instance, consider these questions:

- ⸫ Who oversees the laws?
- ⸫ Do we designate special people to keep and maintain the laws and rules? Why them? How are they educated? How to we judge their inner experience of

Yeshua and the Kingdom? How do we remove them from offices of power when necessary and how do we know we should?

- ❓ What is the fundamental difference between a law keeper and a law breaker?
- ❓ What is the cost of breaking a law or rule? Who sets this price?
- ❓ Who is in step and who is out of step with the majority? Does that make them "wrong" if they are out of step?
- ❓ Is the rule more important than a person's experience?
- ❓ Is a law itself relative, based on time, gender, age, geographical location, local custom and thus impossible to make universal?
- ❓ And so on…

As you can see from this short list, laws and rules become binding elements, not a path to freedom. In a sense, they create a false sense of relationship in the form of tribal membership. This false relationship may in fact hinder a person's ability to search the Imaginal Realm within and find that life-giving Presence of Yeshua and the eyes and ears that delight in the Kingdom.

Walking forth and spreading the news of Yeshua and the Kingdom does seem to put his students in an interesting bind. How do people teach without creating institutions, "right information" vs "wrong information", authentic teachers vs inauthenticity, leadership positions, inner circles, on and on? It does call for a very light hand, a way that is more about living as Yeshua than "teaching about Yeshua".

As we shall see toward the end of this study, it's very plausible that the male disciples deeply misunderstood the nature of the call to go forth and proclaim the life and teachings of Jesus. The ramifications of that misunderstanding are with us to this day.

Responsive Poem:

Stand naked before a mirror—

do you flinch,

voices in your head saying,

"you should be a size 5,

with more lustrous hair

without glasses,

with better makeup,

in better shape?"

Endless the realities imposed by

impostors

of your Self.

Are you flooded with memories?

Words rooted in rules,

in social correctness,

in theology,

and as they pass through you,

do you label each moment,

identifying with "good" or "bad"?

Endless the realities imposed by

impostors

of your Self.

Do you bow down to a parade of powerful Others,

teachers, parents, spouse, priests, media personalities,

ghostly voices molding your own features,

blurring the bones of your precious face?

Endless are the realities imposed by

impostors

of your Self.

Do you worry about being alone,

outside, cast out,

dying apart?

Is this image, bound in glass and a wood frame,

the only fragile, imperfect, impossibly marred Real?

Endless are the realities imposed by

impostors

of your Self.

Reach out and touch your image,

fingertip meeting fingertip,

then step back.

Close your eyes, quiet your mind.

Let your own touch fall on

your belly,

your heart,

your lips,

blessing even

the crown of your head,

and

listen with ears that hear,

for endless are the realities imposed by

impostors

of your Self.

Engaging the Text:

1. How does a teaching that asks students not to keeping adding rules or laws jive with modern expressions of Christianity? Be concrete.

2. Why would this form of Christianity be difficult to institutionalize? Are there shadows evident to you in this teaching? Explain?

3. How do laws and rules help create relationships? How do they hinder relationships?

4. How do you image and interact with "Yeshua within you?" What techniques or states of consciousness do you utilize to realize this relationship?

5. How much of your understanding and relationship with Yeshua is based on others saying, in some or many words, "he's here" or "he's over there." Put another way, how has ritual, theology, scriptural sources, human teachers, and so on affected how you *expect* to encounter Yeshua's Presence or the Kingdom? Explain.

Chapter 8

Translation:

"Yeshua's students were upset and wept bitterly. "How are we supposed to walk forth and announce the Kingdom and the message of the Son of Humanity? He was not spared from death, so how will we be spared?"

(Page 9, Lines 6-11)

Musings:

I feel, with this passage, just how frightened the disciples of the Teacher really were. Despite the presence of the risen Yeshua with them only moments before, the horrors of physical death reign supreme in this visceral response. His continued presence, promised to them, does not allay their terror. They are still locked deeply in a world with beginnings and endings, where Matter feels like the only reality, and the leave taken by their leader is a complete and total "goodbye."

Grief and fear take time to work through. Even though Yeshua promised to be with them always, that they would find him within, and had pointed out that death is not the end, this is too huge a paradigm shift to make. They can't access "ears that hear", and that is a big part of being human, a child of both matter and spirit.

If we step back from the terror and take a more bifocal view, we see the terrible power of being locked into just one way of understanding reality. Without the ability to use the lenses of both relative and ultimate reality, the disciples cannot access the presence of their teacher, nor can they apply his teachings to their own experience and lives. Often, we when are trapped in the throes of simply living in relative reality, the root of all our thoughts and actions and emotions tends to be a pervading fear. It's the fear of being wholly alone, outside the pale of our chosen or familial tribe. It's the fear of concrete endings, as well as the fear we haven't "lived enough" or "collected enough" or "gotten enough love." It's the fear of not being heard, of not connecting, of (as the late Rev. Dr. Tom Thresher loved to say) "dying alone under a bridge". The individual self becomes a light with a very dark hole in the center. Fear causes anger, violence, depression and a whole host of states, emotions, thoughts and actions. Scratch any of these within yourself and see if you can identify the lurking face of fear.

The message of the cross is a powerful one—you must hang between the arms of eternity and linear historical time, your heart (not your head) at this intersection. You must die to the part of yourself that clings to *either* path—that of Matter and Relative Reality AND that of eternity or Ultimate Reality. Incarnation demands nothing less than this—but the real gift is *the ability to place fear into context.* Fear will continue to exist, right along with "Father, why have you forsaken me?" But it is held more lightly because of the presence of Ultimate Reality. The disciples cannot imagine hanging their hearts in this intersection. Blinded by grief, by terror and by a deep fear in their guts, they are bound and, in a sense, already partaking of death.

The students' reaction helps us to clarify the very real "cost" of not walking and seeing as Yeshua did. It stands as a stark teaching of crying in the darkness when we cannot or will not simply turn to the light.

Responsive Poem:

(A Re-Interpretation of a Poem often attributed to

St. Francis of Assisi)

Abba, lets us together play the music of your peace.
In its sweet notes, we find the way beyond the dualities
of hatred and love,
of injury and pardon,
of doubt and faith,
of despair and hope,
of darkness and light,
of sadness and joy.

Let our shared breath affirm
we are the misunderstood, the understood and energy of
understanding,
the lover, the beloved, and the energy of loving,
the giver, the receiver and the energy of the Gift,
the pardoner, the pardoned and the pardoning,

Let us, together,
sing forth eternity,
both beyond and yet within
this straight line
of living,
of dying.

Amen.

Engaging the Text:

1. Throughout your day, notice your thoughts and passing emotional states that you are apt to label "negative". If you look deeply at them, what is their root cause?

2. How do you understand the symbolism of the cross? How do you *apply it* to your life, as more than a neat idea? Look at a collection of crosses, including those with Yeshua present in the middle and those without. Is there a different message in each? In what ways are they the same? How would Mary or Yeshua in this Gospel talk about the cross? Would they think of it as a powerful symbol at all?

3. What do you think (or in your experience) is the dominant fear of human beings? How does Yeshua address this fear, both here, as well as in the Bible? What do you think keeps us from applying those teachings, day in and day out?

4. Are you comfortable standing "alone" or apart from the crowd, from "your" political party, your church or even your friends? Where does this fear come from?

5. When you first read this passage today, what was your initial response? Did your response change as you read more deeply into the text? The text took me into a consideration of the cross for a time—where did it take you? Explain.

Chapter 9

Translation:

Mary rose and moved amongst them, speaking with compassion to all who were gathered. "Dry your tears and find your balance. Yeshua's presence will be with you all and remind you of your center. We should rejoice for he has prepared each of us to Stand as Single Ones." She helped them recall what they had learned from Yeshua, and they began to more calmly discuss the meaning of his teachings.

(Page 9, Lines 12-20)

Musings:

Here we see Mary in action as a leader and as a nurturing (compassionate) presence within the structure of Yeshua's community. She embodies both his healing and his relational ability, as well as reminds his students that Yeshua's teaching had always pointed to this moment, when they would have to Stand as complete human beings.

The passage is remarkable, given the cultural constraints on the women of this time and place. We can almost feel the presence and wisdom of Yeshua within Mary, showing us how to be a whole or unified human being. Her very "presence" is strong enough to calm the atmosphere, to dry tears, and help everyone back to a different kind of consciousness, despite the tremendous traumas and revelations that had assailed them all.

Responsive Poem:

Ihidaya.

Anthropos.

I took the terms for a walk with my dog,

the winter wind spinning up

little white whirlwinds in the driveway,

the snow stinging my eyes.

I paused when I spotted two crows,

snuggling high overhead on a bounding oak branch.

Their beaks touched now and again,

wings tried to cover each other,

and then the flock flashed overhead,

and the air itself threw them back into the sky,

mixing them with the crowd of darting black shapes.

Yeshua.

Mary Magdalene.

Incarnation.

Engaging the Text:

1. Did Mary's stepping into Yeshua's usual role surprise you? Explain. Take some time to research how women were usually seen and treated by the Temple culture of Judaism of this time. Look also at how women were treated in Greek and Roman cultures.

2. Do you think Mary is acting as if Yeshua was a savior or a teacher who wanted his students to walk as he did in the world and beyond? How do you define savior? How do you define "spiritual teacher"?

3. Notice there is no mention of any kind of substitution or sacrificial theology (Yeshua died for our sins). What are the ramifications for modern Christianity if we take this image of the life of Yeshua and Mary to heart?

4. Why do you think humans tend to "follow and glorify" a teacher rather than seek to be like that teacher? Can you find any Biblical references that support Yeshua was encouraging his students to learn to Stand and be "whole human beings" rather than simply worship him? How do you feel about Mary's level of ability to Stand, show compassion, nurture, and heal?

5. How would you describe your center or balance point when the world seems to be falling apart? How do you access it and live out of it?

Chapter 10

Translation:

*Peter addressed Mary, "We know Yeshua loved you
differently from other women. Share with us anything he
conveyed to you that perhaps we haven't heard before."*

(Page 10, Lines 1-7)

Musings:

This is one of the classic lines that recent advocates of a
marriage or physical relationship between Yeshua and Mary
point to in their books and teachings. I'm not going to say it
never happened, only we will never know for certain. To me,
personally, it's enough to know Yeshua and Mary shared a
different relationship, an intimacy of spirit. That idea
touches me, as both a woman and seeker, most deeply. It's
also sound to make the claim of a deep spiritual teacher-
student relationship, based on the Gospels of Mary
Magdalene, Philip and Thomas, as well as a deeper reading
of the canonical texts.

Notice the passage can be read that Mary wasn't an *object*;
she had a spiritual presence that transcended any gender
designation. *Yeshua didn't look at her like men in his
culture, at that point in time, tended to look at women.* This
is the kind of message that rocks the foundations of modern
Christianity. Again, if you take the time to look at
interactions between Yeshua and women, you can see how
his connection with Mary may have rippled out into his
treatment of women in general. His message about the

Father, Reality, compassion, healing and more encompassed not just men, but the whole of humanity. He elevated women to spiritual equals, and this Gospel certain illustrations that Mary was the only disciple who truly understood him completely.

Mary is sometimes called "the Apostle to the Apostles", based primarily on her status of being the first to see Yeshua in his risen form and it is she who carries the message to the men that he had appeared to her and was "ascending to my Father and your Father, to my God and your God" (John 20:17). Yet, she is never included as an apostle in the "official" lists. Today, we are called to rethink that short-sightedness and see her as she plainly was—the first-most and intimate student of the teacher we call Yeshua.

Notice that not only had she heard the usual teachings given by Yeshua to all his students and is able to manifest them (as in the passage before this one), Peter here asks for the words the disciples did NOT hear! This certainly points to the "different" sort of relationship shared by Yeshua and Mary. This text, then, serves as a retort to those who would claim women have no place in church leadership—*Mary is the only student who understood and acted out of the teachings of Yeshua, and she also was known by the others to have had access to the words of their Master they had not been party to.* Sadly, hers is the voice the later orthodoxy would silence—the beginnings of that silencing by insidious cultural norms can be seen later in this text as well as in the Gospel of Thomas.

Responsive Poem:

In 2008,

a mainline Protestant church

banned women from the pulpit and church leadership.

I read the words, shaking my head.

Funny, how we can twist

Biblical writings and other sources into

a dogma,

a creed,

a law,

that looks suspiciously like a mirror image of

our hatreds, our politics, our power bases, our agendas.

It helps if the Other is easily identified—

a color of skin,

a nationality

a gender,

rather than meeting them relationally

as capable and intelligent,

as compassionate and tender,

as creative and visionary.

May we forgive each other

when we so clearly

miss the mark.

Engaging the Text:

1. Take the time to read passages in the Bible where Yeshua interacts with women, not just Mary Magdalene. What do you notice?

2. Why do you think it's easier to objectify others based on their outer shells? From where does this tendency arise? Can you see it at work within you? Explain. If you choose to look deeply, remember not to condemn yourself, but rather, simply bring to conscious what lives within you.

3. Why might the church, after the Council of Nicaea, find this Gospel a difficult pill to swallow?

4. Compare the relationship of Yeshua and Mary with Radha and Krishna in Hinduism, with Shiva and Shakti in Tantric teachings, with Buddha and his women followers (look also at the relationship between Buddha and his wife and son.) Read the Song of Songs in the Bible. What are the similarities and differences you observe?

5. In your opinion, is a sexual relationship between Yeshua and Mary a vital part of understanding them and their teachings? Take up your journal and consider the question.

Chapter 11

Translation:

Mary replied to Peter, "I will share with you what has been veiled from you." And then she began to teach.

(Page 10, Lines 7-9)

Musings:

She began to teach! Read all the translations that exist—you will find the same energy. Mary Magdalene steps up into the role of Yeshua for the gathered students, with authority and strength. Peter has asked her to do this (and this is remarkable for a character who tends to stiffen and react rather than ask for clarity). So, we can be reasonably assured that the apostles knew she was a strong and able keeper of Yeshua's teachings.

Also notice that Mary herself is aware that she has been given access to information that the others have not. She has received a different *kind* transmission from Yeshua (as we will soon see) as well as different content. These factors again point to the intimacy between Mary as a spiritual seeker and her *rabboni*.

Responsive Poem:

Mary, can I catch your voice?

Can I hear you,

through

the wind-driven sand?

Your dry words rasp as

static

when I tune in with this damaged instrument

of orthodox theology.

Let me adjust my batteries,

fiddle with settings.

I'm still playing with the bass and treble,

hoping I'll

catch strains beyond worn ideas of

prostitute,

repentant sinner,

ignorant woman

groveling at the feet

of men.

I'd like to ignore

cultures and years and my own

skin color and education—

social and otherwise.

In truth, though,

they contribute to the background din.

Head close to the speaker,

tipping my head,

shutting my eyes,

my heart picks up the vibration

clear and undefended.

I'll try to hum it all

later.

Engaging the Text:

1. What elements of our culture, education and more keep us from "hearing" Mary today? Be concrete.

2. How do you feel about receiving teachings from a woman, even if you are a woman? What comes up in your heart and in your thoughts?

3. Go to the Bible, as well as the Gospel of Thomas and notice Peter's role through-out. You can search Bible online sites using his name. Given what you find, how do you feel about Mary accepting Peter's request for teachings? Come back to this question towards the end of this book!

4. Should keepers of deep spiritual information attempt to share those insights when asked? Why or why not? The Bible and the Gospel of Thomas warns (paraphrasing), "don't throw your pearls before swine". How do you interpret this insight?

5. What are your personal sources of wisdom? What spiritual questions do you ask yourself or others? How do you know when the answers you receive are "correct for you"?

Chapter 12

Translation:

Mary said, "I encountered Yeshua in a vision and I conveyed to him I was aware of his Presence there."

"He said to me, 'you are blessed because this vision did not trouble you. For where the Presence of Spirit (Nous) is, there is the treasure.'"

(Page 10, Lines 10-16)

Musings:

Do take some time and consult other translations of this passage, especially how I've translated the vision as a connection between Mary and Yeshua's Presence of Spirit. It's sometimes conveyed as "mind", sometimes as "heart", sometimes as Nous (a slippery word meaning "divine Reason", common sense, intellect, and so forth). Here in the West, we don't have a good way to describe the "third" presence in encounters like "when two or more are gathered in my name, I AM (God is) there with them" (Matthew 18:20). How do you gather in a name? Does that mean you simply come together as "Christians"? Or does it point to the idea that the Name means the presence Yeshua conveyed to the world, the great I AM? Did Mary have that kind of meeting with her teacher?

Yeshua, through his student Mary, authorizes and even praises her ability to connect with him outside the realm of physical presence. Interestingly, if you go back and read the Bible carefully, you will be able to identify distinct visionary and shamanic events throughout the text. Mary's "vision" therefore is wholly in keeping with her culture and time in history. Abraham, Jacob, Joseph, Samuel, Solomon, Daniel, Zacharias, Pilate's wife, Ananias, Peter, Paul, and John to name just a few major characters all experienced visions. If we take the word *nous* to partially mean "common sense or intellect," I think we need to consider as well that visions were an acceptable way to receive messages and entertain divine presence in Mary's world. They were part and parcel of how to encounter God.

While we may flinch at the idea of a visionary experience conveying valid teachings, people in Mary's time wouldn't necessarily have had the same reaction. Yeshua praises her ability to not be startled by him, and indeed points out that the very "treasure" he is offering everyone can be best found by accessing this specific kind of consciousness, this Nous or Presence, that arises between the meeting of two hearts and minds.

It's important to understand that this vision is not a dream, not a daydream, not an ecstatic encounter separate from logic and language, not imagination or creative visualization. It's a meeting of two hearts in clarity and communion, much more like the experience of modern core shamanic practitioners when they meet their spirit guides on shamanic journeys. It requires a completely different order of consciousness, one that Yeshua himself calls a "treasure".

Responsive Poem:

The doorway is always present—
wondering where the hole at the base
of a leaning tree might take you;
touching the surface of the lake,
your fingertips bridging sky and water;
hearing music, poetry, scripture, myth;
gazing through a telescope,
through a microscope,
into the eyes of your child.
Always, the invitation
blows past your nose,
tickles the hairs on the back of your neck,
leans in for a feathery butterfly kiss.
RSVP if you want,
but never miss a chance to duck through.

Engaging the Text:

1. What role have visions played in your own life? How have you received information about the efficacy of visions?

2. Were you surprised how often visions have been a part of major episodes within the Bible?

3. Create a piece of art, music, dance or writing that captures the visionary experience.

4. When did visions as a valid and accepted means to understand the Divine become separated from the consciousness that we call rational, logical, and so forth? Do some homework and see if you can find a point in history when this happened for much of the Christian world. Are there still forms/instances of Christianity that embrace visions even today?

5. Does Mary's claim she spoke with Yeshua in a vision put you off or intrigue you? Explain.

Chapter 13

Translation:

"Rabonni, when someone sees and hears you in a vision, does the experience arise from the soul or the spirit?"

Yeshua replied, "These visions do not arise from the soul or the spirit, but rather from a different form of consciousness, the nous between the two, and this is which...."

(Page 10, Lines 17-25)

Musings:

ARRRRRHHGGGGGGGHHHHH! This is the section where our extant texts contain damage, and Yeshua doesn't finish his explanation about how visions operate *within* the human being. Until another archeological miracle turns up, we must work with what we have. In the next chapter, we'll be faced with Mary's vision mid-stream, parts of her revelation silenced by the missing text. Some authors have pointed to a deliberate excising of these sections, but the fact is, we have what we have, no matter how the pages were damaged or went missing. The gap certainly invites us into creatively working with what is not there—the very exercise of a spiritual seeker. But it will always remain a mystery and tragedy.

Mary begins this section on Page 10 with questions to clarify the visions she has experienced. She is trying to define if the experience arises within her soul or if is it "given" from outside of herself.

Yeshua points out that neither concept is correct. Rather, the meeting of the soul and Spirit create a third state of consciousness, which is the vision. It's intimate, a dance between the individual and Reality, a kind of *participatory incarnation*. Therefore, the messages received, the presence acknowledged is "real"—indeed, it has its own life, born of the soul and Mystery interpenetrating each other and creating the third "person" of the originating elements.

This entire work refutes bodily resurrection, but balances that with the way we come into a living relationship with Yeshua even today. *Like Mary, we are called not to "cling" to the matter that was the Teacher, but rather, meet him where soul and spirit create a Presence.*

Responsive Poem:

I know this movement of something

more than consensual mind.

(Look in yourself—you will find it, too!)

I have stared through the eyes of my science fiction
character,

a creation,

an individual,

who grins frankly back at me.

I have walked a trail with a poet

who died this past summer,

and still see things she points out on the way.

I have argued with saints and mystics,

nodded along with spirit guides, chatting,

and even entered old houses and found myself

filled

with what was and what could be.

Each time, a birth.

Each time, a participatory incarnation.

Engaging the Text:

1. Why would this idea of being able to access Yeshua through visions be frightening to the orthodoxy as it was developing in Rome?

2. Do you find yourself mistrusting any information that comes to you through someone else's vision? Explain. What does that suggest about the spiritual journey and your own relationship with Yeshua?

3. How did you feel when Yeshua's teachings cut off? Based on his partial answer, do you think you can access what is not said there?

4. What are the differences between a vision, a daydream, a hallucination, a night time dream, imagination and a creative act? In what way do they work together in this thing we call "mind"?

5. Does this passage harken toward "Bridal Chamber Theology?" Do your research and develop your answer.

Chapter 14

Translation:

"Desire spoke, 'I did not observe you descend, yet now I see you ascending. Why are you lying to me, since you are mine?'

The soul replied, 'I was aware of you, and I know you did not see me or know me. You thought the clothes I wore were my Self. And so, you never recognized me.'

Once it had spoken, the soul departed in joy."

(Page 15, Lines 1-12)

Musings:

We enter the conversation mid-stream, and with no speaker signified in name. But because Mary was sharing her vision of what Yeshua had conveyed to her, I believe, along with author and scholar Cynthia Bourgeault, that the person relating the story is he. Cynthia presents an interesting theory in her book, *The Meaning of Mary Magdalene: Discovering the Woman at the Heart of Christianity.* Because the Gospel of Mary Magdalene occurs immediately after Yeshua's encounter with her at the tomb, this may be a record, in his voice, of what happened to him after death. It's a fascinating hypothesis, and it certainly resonates with my heart, but of course it's very difficult to logically and factually prove. I leave it to your own good intuitions!

The message here, though, is fascinating. Desire (sometimes translated as *Craving)* serves as both a character and concept.

In the vision, this kind of consciousness is given a life so Yeshua's soul can speak directly to it. It's a lovely literary device, used to point out what was unconscious before, but was indeed "alive" and functioning in some part of the mind or soul. Desire and craving hook us constantly, sometimes in very subtle ways and sometimes in terrible and life-changing manners. In almost every spiritual tradition, when we move *with* the current of Craving, we *become* it.

But Yeshua's soul retorts that what was hooked was merely a set of clothes, a mask, an image rather than an icon. While Desire was sure it owned the *soul*, it was only grasping a mirage, the manufactured and socially conditioned *ego*.

In Buddhism and some of the Yogic traditions of India, as well as some of the teachings of Sufism, part of the practice is becoming conscious of the power of desire and craving, and how it is part of the energy that causes human beings to suffer in a variety of unpleasant ways. Part of meditation and analysis of how the mind functions is learning to fully see desire, to understand it as a form of passing thought and emotion, and to bring it to full consciousness. This is the newly dawning movement of mind and soul in the *Gospel of Mary Magdalene*, and in Buddhism and Yogic philosophy, we see a similar picture: "we" are not our Craving and our Desire. We are not owned by this emotion-laden energy and thought—it adheres to or "recognizes" our internal clothes, masks and egos rather than our True Selves.

Once we "know" this in a deep way, we are free. Our soul, our Self, is filled with the joy of a freedom that was always and forever available.

Responsive Poem:

Scratch the itch in your back-brain-

the one craving chocolate cake,

the one yearning for a new nightie,

the one desiring

something

anything,

always.

Hold your fingernails up to your glasses.

Can you see the hooks,

sunk in so deep they bleed?

My words alone make you shudder.

I know they

drive you to turn away

and dream of spring,

hope for a new car,

yearn for a trip to the craft store.

Stay here.

Feel.

Be free for a moment,

or for eternity.

Engaging the Text:

1. With your journal in hand, give your own desires or cravings a voice and character. You can even draw its face, so you have an image to work with. Then ask it questions that come to mind, like "where do you live?" "How were you born within me?" "What is your function within me?"

2. One of the great paradoxes of spiritual practice of any kind is that we must desire or crave enlightenment or relationship with Mystery. Do you think craving has other "functions" that help us down the paths of our lives? As you look at what you discover, can you really name Desire or Craving bad or evil? Explain.

3. Take the time to draw the "clothes" of your soul or list some of the veils you have become aware of. Talk or write a poem about how you feel when you become aware of some of these layers. For instance, I am very aware that my degrees, my books, and so forth sometimes get mixed up with who I am at a soul level—by naming them, I become conscious that I am not these things. They are masks, outfits, costumes. In the naming, you bring them to consciousness so you can be acutely aware of them and that consciousness eases you toward freedom and authenticity.

4. Do some research about how Buddhism, mystical Judaism, Yogic traditions and Sufism work with the concept of desire or craving. Compare what you find to this passage in the *Gospel of Mary Magdalene.*

Thomas Merton, Meister Eckhart and St. Teresa of Avila from the Christian mystical tradition are also interesting to explore and compare to this text. Your research will lead to yet more voices, if you have an interest. The teachings about bringing what is unconscious to consciousness, even in Christianity, are enormous and powerful! Finally, dive into Transpersonal Psychology for a bit for even more ways to encounter the energy of desire and craving.

5. What are the differences between "soul" and the "True Self" (coined by Thomas Merton) and "enlightenment?" Where do the concepts intersect?

Chapter 15

Translation:

"The third Questioner, named Ignorance, examined the soul and asked, 'Where do you think you are headed? Where is your discernment? For you are chained by wickedness. I can see it!'"

"And the soul replied, 'I have not delivered myself up for judgement. Yes, I have been bound, but I never put anything or anyone else in chains. I was not seen or heard, but I observed that the Cosmos, all that takes physical form or the subtler substance of thought or emotion, dissolves.'"

(Page 15, Lines 13-25)

Musings:

Yet another "inner judge" steps forward, this one named "Ignorance". Like a Medieval morality play, the Gospel of Mary creates a "character" out of thought processes that limit and deride the basic clear awareness of the soul. Here the soul faces that voice within that calls us to examine ourselves harshly, to bind us with our own inner judgement. This is a subtle teaching indeed, which is why the conversation here is between the "soul" and "Ignorance"—it is a turning and facing the conditioned and dualistic part of our minds and hearts that not only bind us, but also serve as judge, jury and executioner. But naming this "ignorance" is a gentle nod to its constructed and ephemeral nature. Ignorance, like "missing the mark", can be addressed and transformed into wisdom.

This is particularly poignant when we recall that Yeshua asked his students *to lay down no new laws*. He was pointing them to the surface face of Ignorance, the tendency to classify "evil", "sin" and the attempts to legislate and chain us and others without really understanding the movements of consciousness within.

The Soul replies to Ignorance that it doesn't judge, so how can it be judged? Yes, you can catch this same echo in the Bible: "Judge not, lest thee be judged," (Matthew 7:1). Here, that command goes far beyond the world of matter and thought, into the very center of our being. The most terrible judge within us is our own Ignorance! When we create new laws or prohibitions, then we manifest that Ignorance and even inflict it upon others.

Part of not being bound to matter or ideas like "judging" or "wickedness" is once again the insight that relative reality is constructed, that all things in heaven and earth fall apart and dissolve. Here, the soul has recognized Ignorance, and found it is not chained, but rather, completely and radically *free*. The soul does not judge—it's totally beyond duality, the right-wrong, sacred-profane, bound-free dichotomies.

Responsive Poem:

I ache with you.

You have absorbed the worlds through your skin:

You echo with "less-than".

You are bound,

by skin color,

by gender,

by age

by race.

Every action you take,

rattles your dear chains over the bones of your face,

the line of your shoulders,

and people mirror back to you

what you present to them.

You wear glasses with bars,

seeing the whole world

inner and outer,

within a self-imposed prison.

You put on headphones

loud with messages

reinforcing and strengthening

social models, ideas, disciplines, correctness.

Lift your chin up,

I beg you,

and stare Ignorance in the face.

Judge not, lest ye be judge, jury and executioner

for your own sweet, joy-rooted Self.

Engaging the Text:

1. Take some time and explore the role of "ignorance" in Buddhist and Yogi and Sufi thought. Compare what you find to this section of the Gospel of Mary Magdalene.

2. Research *Medieval morality plays* on the internet or at your local library. Does the literary device you observe in them differ from or operate in the same way the Gospel of Mary Magdalene uses it? Explain.

3. What role does "Ignorance", as the judging function within yourself, play in your own spiritual journey?

4. Where does Ignorance come from? Make a list of ways we internalize the judge. Does it help you to see this list? Or, as in the Gospel of Thomas, does the list trouble you? Explain.

5. Do you believe you have a "soul" or, as Buddhists believe, do you think everything about our existence is empty? (Be careful not to fall into Nihilism here!) Is Soul another way to "name" states of consciousness? Why or why not? What does Transpersonal Psychology say about the soul? What function does it serve?

Chapter 16

Translation:

"Freed from Ignorance, the soul then found itself in a new territory, the home of Wrath. It bore seven manifestations—Darkness, Craving, Ignorance, Attraction to Death, Clinging to Matter, False Wisdom of Matter, and the False Wisdom of Wrath. They pressed near the soul, asking, 'Where are you coming from, murderer of humans? Where do you think you are headed, destroying wanderer?'"

"The soul answered, 'That which has tried to bind me has been slain, that which pressed hard around me has fallen away; I am free of craving and ignorance. I am released from a world that was a prison, forgotten and time-bound, with the help of a deeper and subtler world. Now, I am timeless, resting in silence.'"

Having said all this, Mary fell silent, expressing the deep quiet of the vision in which her teacher had spoken to her.

(Page 16, Lines 1-19 and Page 17, Lines 1-8)

Musings:

The veils of the soul continue to blow away, and its own clarity draws it closer and closer to its center and source. This last set of characterizations, like beings in a Tibetan Bardo state encountered at death, press the soul, the energy of Wrath splintering into its constituent parts. Rather than being bound or fleeing, the soul stands firm. Notice that it refuses to engage each characterization at this point, but rather gives a birth-cry of freedom and awakening. It knows it has broken the paradigm of matter and humanity as limited and existing in time only, with the help of a different kind of seeing, a totally new understanding of life. By becoming conscious of the Ultimate Reality, Relative Reality alone no longer binds the soul. It apprehends eternity, the richness of rest and silence—the nothing, the Emptiness that is simply *everything*.

Mary has absorbed this vision deeply, and her own stillness of being reflects what the Master has shown her. This kind of transmission of consciousness from her Rabonni to herself again underlines the intimate connection between Mary Magdalene and Yeshua. Because of the nous linking them, his experience becomes her own. She could, like Paul, say "No longer I, but it is Christ who lives in me," (Galatians, 2:20).

Responsive Poem:

I sketched Wrath's face

on my digital drawing pad—

hair roped with jealousy,

each tooth a remembered hurt,

eyes looking for conquests and accolades,

a black tongue,

passing along lies.

Then, consciously,

I hit the undo button

again and yet again

until the screen waited,

patient

for the birth of new worlds.

Form is Emptiness,

Emptiness is Form,

right where my fingertips

rest on mobile keys.

Engaging the Text:

1. Draw a picture of the Wrath, bringing in the subtle "characters" Yeshua shared with Mary. What did the artwork teach you?

2. How does this Gospel change the way Yeshua is usually portrayed by Christianity?

3. Take the time to learn about the *Tibetan Book of the Dead* and the *Bardo* states—how is this like Mary's vision? How is it different? Read Buddha's awakening experience as well as the *Parinirvana Sutra* (Buddha's last teaching) and compare it to this gospel. What do you notice?

4. Does "resting in timelessness" and silence resonate with the practice of mindfulness meditation? Explain.

5. Is this image of what happens to the soul at death give you any comfort, as it seemed to help Mary? How does it compare to the concept of heaven as you understand it?

Chapter 17

Translation:

"Andrew said, 'I don't know what the rest of you heard, but I don't believe Yeshua himself said these things. The ideas are too strange and different from what he taught us."

(Page 17, Lines 9-13)

Musings:

The first man to comment on Mary's revelation illustrates humanity's inherent resistance to hearing a new idea. In this case, Andrew is internally comparing what he had heard in the past to this new set of teachings. What is fascinating about his comments is the idea that Yeshua's experience of what happens to the soul probably hadn't been taught to the students before this moment *because the Rabbi himself had not experienced it yet.* Mary bridges the death event and the resurrection event, and Andrew cannot make the jump. It doesn't jive with who he remembered Yeshua *was.*

It also harkens back to the reason why Peter asked Mary to teach in the first place—she was given privy information by Yeshua because of their spiritual intimacy. On one level, the apostles recognized she had been given different teachings from what they had often heard, or she had understood the common teachings at a much deeper level. But here, Andrew cannot condone the ideas that would elevate Mary to a bearer of new revelations from Yeshua. As we shall soon see, Peter becomes even more resistant to her vision, reverting to his usual patriarchal and materialistic ignorance.

Responsive Poem:

The rock, pried out of the frozen driveway,

shared a song

written in the slow ridged curl

of a fossil.

The ice,

piling four feet high at the water's edge,

wrote a poem in

light and trapped air bubbles.

The Northern Pike,

drawn from the deep,

opened its toothed jaw,

a universe unfolding endlessly

in its maw.

Rock, ice and a too-small fish—

who knew.

Who Knew?

Engaging the Text:

1. What biases can you list that get in the way of hearing this gospel? For instance, I might include orthodox teachings of Christianity, a distrust of visions as "real" teachings, and so forth. Make the list as complete as you are able. Then, imagine you could quiet these sources of judgement by asking "what if..." So, I would ask myself, "What if this was the orthodox Christian tradition?" or "What if visions revealed new teachings?" See what shifts within.

2. What are Andrew's biases? Based on this Gospel, where is he stuck?

3. How does getting stuck in dogma, teachings, and traditional ways of doing things prevent spiritual growth? In what ways do such things support spiritual growth?

4. How do you *feel* about Andrew in this part of the Gospel of Mary? Do you feel confident he is really teaching the full message of Yeshua when he goes forth to spread the Good News? Explain.

5. As we can tell from the early pages of this gospel, the apostles were very frightened about going back out into the world. How would fear affect their ability to hear Mary's revelation?

Chapter 18

Translation:

"And Peter said, 'Why would Yeshua speak in this way to a woman but not to us? Are we not taught from birth to not listen to women? Why would he choose her to reveal such teachings?"

(Page 17, Lines 14-20)

Musings:

Go back and read again how Peter was the student who asked for the teachings from Mary. Notice he not only seemed to understand Mary and Yeshua had a different sort of relationship, he also asked explicitly for those intimate teachings. When Andrew doesn't seem to be able to comprehend her vision's message, Peter immediately sides with his fellow male student, citing his time's patriarchal and societal injunctions against women, and clearly feeling jealous of the place Mary had in Yeshua's life.

Peter is often used in Biblical stories as a kind of mirror for how we approach both Yeshua and faith. His rash actions, loose tongue and frequent misunderstandings of Yeshua's example and teachings help us see our own inner Peter. (He's called the Tempter by Yeshua in Matthew 16:23: "Get thee behind me, Tempter!" when Peter names Yeshua the Messiah after the classic Transfiguration vision.) However, it doesn't make his words any easier to hear in this gospel. Like denying Yeshua himself three times because it seemed the "safe" thing to do, we again see Peter holding to the strictures and traditions of his time, as well as to his own sense of egoic self-preservation.

It's a poignant place in this gospel—the beginnings of a clear death toll for teachings given by women, of the veracity of visions, and of the subtle ways of understanding Yeshua as a bringer of wisdom and transformation of consciousness. Peter is locked into his culture, his materiality, his patriarchal ideology, and sadly, he is an example of the kind of men that took the message of Yeshua out into the world. If Peter's role is to stand for all the ways we miss the mark, we are certainly called to re-examine our reactions to both Mary and this gospel.

Responsive Poem:

On the cushion,

I fall away—

body, breath, mind.

But something also enters,

some soft broadening

to experiences:

my thumb rubbing sand

from the smooth surface of sea glass;

the warm scent of pine tree sap;

the curious tip of my dog's head;

the graveled sound of the raven sandpapering the wood;

the sweet slip of chocolate coffee over my tongue.

Invitations to

revelation

through

relationship.

Engaging the Text:

1. In what ways do you think your ability to accept new paradigms and ideas is limited by your gender, your chosen faith and friends, your economic status and so forth?

2. Go back and read all the parts of the Bible where Peter is mentioned. Then create a picture, a poem or piece of music that captures his message for you. Compare the Biblical Peter to this Peter. How are they alike? How are they different?

3. Have you ever asked for spiritual teachings, then found yourself rejecting and escaping the message, returning to what is familiar and safe? Why do you think this is a normal human reaction to new information or new ways of seeing reality?

4. Yeshua's teachings are deeply relational, both in the Bible and in texts like the Gospel of Thomas. In what ways do humans back away from intimate relationship? Why does this happen?

5. What roles would psychological stress and fear play in both Peter's and Andrew's response to Mary's vision? How do you feel about men like these conveying Yeshua's teachings to the world? What are the ramifications to Christianity when it lost messages like the Gospel of Mary Magdalene?

Chapter 19

Translation:

Mary, crying, answered him, "Peter, do you really believe I made this up? Do you think me capable of lying about our teacher?"

Levi answered Peter, "You have always struggled with anger, Peter. Now you are contending against Mary as if women were adversaries. If Yeshua did not reject her, who are you to do so? His knowledge of her was complete. That's why he loved her, even more than he loved us. We all should ask forgiveness and challenge ourselves to become fully human. That's the only way the Master can live in us. We must continue to develop as he demanded of us, spreading his message while not laying down any new rules or laws other than what he gave us."

When Levi finished speaking, they left that place to begin to teach others.

The Gospel According to Mary Magdalene

(Page 18, Lines 1-21 and Page 19, lines 1-3)

Musings:

There are many reasons Mary might cry here. But one of the most powerful may be the complete loneliness she was feeling. There is nothing worse on the spiritual journey than to find yourself in a paradigm change, when few folk (sometimes even close friends) are capable of understanding what you are experiencing. Ken Wilber, in his work with integral spirituality, mentions that the deeper inward you journey, the more people working on the previous stages will not be able to understand you. Peter and Levi both are still functioning in time, still locked into dualism—the pressures and social expectations of their culture, the literal words of their teacher, the role of women in their time and place all come into play here. They've heard the words, but not with ears that truly hear. Now, they head out to teach what they understood only in part. And so, the message of Yeshua begins to degrade from that moment forward, eventually becoming lost in legalism, dogma, cultural norms and literalism except for the occasional mystical lamp that continues to flare through history and into our present day and age.

While Levi is clearly sympathetic to Mary's feelings, notice he neatly sidesteps the issue of whether the visions were true or not, chiding Peter for his behavior rather than addressing how he felt about the content of Mary's revelation. He clings to the idea of making no more new laws or rules—essentially returning to legalistic dualism. While he seems to sense that there remains a call to transformation, it is an idea only and not an integral part of his spiritual path. Within him, the message is already set in stone, and all further revelation silenced.

For Mary, who has lost her intimate and beloved master in physical manifestation, whose visions have been discounted, who finds herself heir to Yeshua's deepest teachings yet is not believed, who has nurtured and interacted with her "brothers" and not received that love in turn, who has had to put up with the jealousy and ignorance of people like Peter, the tears are poignant, painful and very likely trigger by more than just her hurt feelings. Silencing her muzzles a part of Yeshua as well.

Such "silencing" is another kind of death of the Master which she must bear alone, unless today we finally have ears that hear.

Responsive Poem:

The drum pictured on my Kindle is black,

cut "U"s, worked in steel,

a ten-note scale or so

it claims.

But on the screen,

passive and silent,

I have nothing to go by,

no sweet or tinny voice,

just dimensions,

weight

manufacturing information

shipping cost and price.

Facts do not sing.

Numbers cannot whisper to my heart.

Mechanics mean nothing.

My restless fingers swish the ad away.

Engaging the Text:

1. Make a list of reasons why you think Mary cried in this passage of the Gospel of Thomas. What did you learn about her?

2. How much credence is given to spiritual experience in most forms of religion? Who decides the veracity of visions, of new ideas and so forth? What is protected by such behavior?

3. What might Christianity have looked like if this gospel had made it into the Bible?

4. Draw an image of Mary or find a way to express her in other mediums, capturing what you have learned about her from this gospel. Is it different from what you may have created before you read this work?

5. What will you take away from this study? How do you think it will affect your own spiritual journey?

Resources for Further Inquiry

The Gospel of Mary Magdalene. *Jean Yves-LeLoup. 2002. Inner Traditions.*

The Gospel of Mary Magdala: Jesus and the First Woman Apostle. *Karen L. King. 2003. Polebridge Press.*

The Luminous Gospels: Thomas, Mary Magdalene and Philip. *Lynn Bauman. 2008. Praxis Press.*

The Meaning of Mary Magdalene: Discovering the Woman at the Heart of Christianity. *Cynthia Bourgeault. 2010. Penguin Random House.*

The Nag Hammadi Scriptures: Revised and Updated Translation of Sacred Gnostic Texts. *Marvin Meyer, Ed. 2008. HarperOne.*

About the Author:

Kim holds a master's degree in comparative religion from Western Michigan University, and completed a year of study at the Iliff School of Theology, specializing in Adult Spiritual Formation and Retreat Management. She is a spiritual director who has also taught in university, college, church and community continuing education settings.

Kim has written 27 books, ranging from poetry to science fiction works, and from comparative religion to children's nature art instruction books. She and her husband co-founded *Family Wild*, a company dedicated to strengthening family relationships through hunting, fishing and nature arts.

Made in the USA
Monee, IL
01 April 2021

64409110R00059